D0915082

Nonsequences

NOnSEQuENCes

o e
N l
s e l F p o E m s
e p
Q o
U e
e M
N s
C
E
s

by Christopher
Middleton

LONGMANS

LONGMANS, GREEN AND CO. LTD
48 Grosvenor Street, London W.1
Associated companies, branches and representatives throughout the world

First published 1965

*Printed in Great Britain by
Western Printing Services Ltd, Bristol*

Contents

Acknowledgements

Acknowledgements are due to the editors of the following periodicals in which certain of these poems have appeared: *Agenda*, *Ambit*, *Burning Deck* (USA), *The Carleton Miscellany* (USA), *Encounter*, *Granta*, *The London Magazine*, *Micromegas* (USA), *The Observer*, *Orient/West* (Japan), *The Paris Review* (USA), *Quagga* (USA), *The Quarterly Review of Literature* (USA), *The Review*, *Stand*, *The Texas Quarterly* (USA), *The Times Literary Supplement*, *Triad* (USA). Nine of the poems were first published in *Penguin Modern Poets No. 4* and two were read in the BBC Third Programme Series 'The Living Poet'.

One inscription for the Berlin Wall

Red earth
of the mountain
red earth dark bodies
twisting and leaping
in their mantillas
of silver and green

Up the staircase
and down
massive accordion
red earth
dark bodies
the walls of stone
hewn fitting

Level to level
weeper-holes
proof
against the burning cloud
erosion breaking
the heart
of a generation

Cabal of cat and mouse

He has a way, the cat, who sits
on the short grass in lamplight.
Him you could appreciate, and more –
how the musky night fits him,
like a glove; how he adapts down there,
below boughs, to his velvet arena.

His, for playing in. A shadow
plodding past his white paws
could be a swad of anything;
except that, as it bolts, he retrieves
and has tenderly couched it,
and must unroll alongside, loving.

His paws dab and pat at it; his
austere head swivels at an angle
to the barrel neck. Prone, he eyes
its minutest move; his haunch relaxing
parades tolerance, for the pose entreats
doubly to play – it is energy

involved, if you like, in a tacit exchange
of selves, as the cat flares up again,
and has seized what he seizes.
And acts proud, does a dance, for it is
his appetite puts all the mouse into a mouse;
the avid mouse, untameable,

bound by so being to concur,
in his bones, with the procedure.
Even the end cannot cancel that.
The shift from play to kill, measured,
is not advertised. He has applied
a reserved gram of tooth power,

to raise this gibbering curt squeal
at last, and now glassily gazes down.
Plunged, barked as if punched,
and has axed his agitator. You heard
soon the headbones crunch; and you shrank,
the spine exploding like a tower in air.

Gaunt man striding

FOR JONATHAN WILLIAMS

Asperity. This rock
pins this hand; from
the other's palm air

spirits a cactus. Rock
heavy as habit. Cactus
throbs and shoots –

it is the pain, love
elemental, gnawing us
animal stars. Clamped,

from shoulder to toe
the body still can
thresh round, wrench.

To rise! You want
man striding, gaunt,
but nimble, dropping

gods in his furrow, now
his famous mushrooms, nights
bruising his great bones

on the desert grains. His
defiance! That being so,
here there is only a hand

under the rock and a hand
the cactus grows from.
To free these – how

burrow the one down
beyond the rock's root,
haul the other up, hose

the whole cactus through it – :
Jonathan Jonathan
keep your pain alive.

The child at the piano

The child at the piano
plinking, planking, plonks.
I stare and stare. Twigs
angle the air with green outside.

Handfuls of notes, all happening at once,
her tunes do not occur; on their backs
round they whizz like stunned wasps; contour
would crush that kind of mass.

Telescoping flukes and faults, their
tenuous terrain dislocates
no spheres I know of. Her index rebounding
off high C beckons no hell boulder up.

The heroics, fatuous, ordain yet
this act's assumption of her whole element.
Boughs of sound swoop through the room,
happily, for her to swing from.

So I call my thought's bluff. My thumb
struts down the keys too, pings
to her plonks, on both white and black notes,
while the green air outside lets us be.

January 1919

What if I know, Liebknecht, who shot you dead.
Tiergarten trees unroll
staggering shadow, in spite of it all.
I am among the leaves; the inevitable
voices
have left nothing to say, the holed head
bleeding across a heap of progressive magazines;
torn from your face,
trees that turned around,
we do not sanctify the land with our wandering.
Look upon our children, they are mutilated.

The cyclops

Since the bellowings
off that hill
predicated some size
above normal

and a vision,
undeflected, deep
and more broad than
ours in our hollow,

our tribute, one beam
from his brow, to scan
our corn, fish, us,
seemed not improper.

We were wrong; drawn
by that monolithic
stare its blank
fondly swallowed

our lies. And the thing
done, we fingered,
as we scoured the hill,
think, from a crevice,

the eye, like a slug,
and it clung, as a slug
clings on a decaying
carrot.

What would you have made of it, Kavafis

What would you have made of it, Kavafis –
he must be standing, in that top room,
the one knee flexed a shade, hand on the sill;
on a table by the window, coils of thread,
needles, patches and other tools of his trade;
but his hair and his nose make him a handsome one
as he glances back, to the peeling door.

All around him, the street below –
in his mind, porters bloom in round caps,
policemen stick their thumbs into their armpits,
linking fingers across silver jacket buttons
as they move along, but gaze at the notices.
A smile passed from a porter to a policeman
is worth his living – or the power of government.
Let them expel his nature, he'll return

to drift above the bar stools,
evenings, when his shop shuts and all that thread
has done its trivial and benign business. Or then
he may saunter down the same street,
to admire, once more, his notice pinned
in the glass case outside the tobacconist's,

not pausing, but smiling, with the grace,
the killing grace of one who keeps a secret,
keeps it (why not)
even from himself when he buckles, offhand, to the task
its message tells of: 'Minute adjustments
to gentlemen's clothing'.

Disturbing the tarantula

The door a maze
of shadow, peach leaves
veining its wood colour,

and cobwebs broken
breathing ah ah
as it is pushed open –

two hands
at a ladder shook
free the tarantula, it slid

black and fizzing to a rung
above eye-level,
knees jack knives,

a high-jumper's, bat mouth
slit grinning
into the fur belly –

helpful: peaches
out there, they keep growing
rounder and rounder

on branches wheeled low
by their weight over
roasted grass blades; sun

and moon, also, evolve
round this mountain
terrace, wrinkling now

with deadly green
emotion: All things
are here, monstrous convulsed

rose (don't anyone
dare come), sounding through
our caves, I hear them.

The runner

She ran to him
  from the ticket barrier
    saying,
      in her language, Are you angry,

are you angry?
  In her blue coat and white
    lambswool cap-
      comforter, cheeks flushed by the

snow, she ran to
  him. So let her run,
    eventually, just
      as late, with just that question

to the one who
  cannot help gathering her
    either
      from the thin night crowd.

In some seer's cloud car

Eyes of slain stag,
Borges the Argentinian,
62, being blind,
flew up to Austin
on tiger's breath, I think,
in some seer's cloud car.

Borges' mother
is 86.
She can't darn or cook.
She feeds him canned soup,
with what tenderness,
and sends the laundry out.

Borges the poet,
by her escorted, steered,
quotes by the yard in living rooms
English saga, German song.
He has it all by heart.
He's honeycombed.

And robust bread
browns in our oven.
We zoom down streets to shop
detergent, checked by signs.
And behold, way below,
the dark town sparkle.

Me, my table groans
under Arp and dictionaries.
60 ungraded exercises,
treatises, a score – when
Borges asks 'What was that word?'
there's not one I remember.

By whale I came here, it seems.
On whale back, past Labrador.
On the *n*th day,
spotted dawn over Dallas
in skies of purple steam,
and ate an egg.

Navajo children
Canyon de Chelly, Arizona

You sprouted from sand,
running, stopping, running;
beyond you tall red
tons of rock rested
on the feathery tamarisk.

Torn jeans, T-shirts
lope and skip, toes drum
and you're coming
full tilt
for the lollipops,

hopefully
arrive, daren't
look, for our stares
(your noses dribble)
prove too rude

in your silence,
can't break, either,
your upturned
monkey faces into smiles.
It's no joke,

as you grope
up, up
to the driver's door, take
them reverently, the
lollipops –

your smallest, too small,
waited three
paces back, shuffling,
then provided,
evidently

by a sister on tiptoe who
takes his hand, helps
unwrap the sugar totem.
And we are swept
on, bouncing,

look back,
seeing walls
dwarf you. But how
could you get any
more thin, small, far.

Lenau's dream

Scares me mad, that dream;
wish I could tell my-
self I slept without

a dream! But what of
these tears pouring down
still, loud throb of heart?

Waking, I was done up.
My handkerchief wet
(had I just buried

someone?). Don't know how
I got hold of it,
and me fast asleep –

but they were there, the
visitors, evil,
I gave them my house

for their feast, then got
off to bed, while they
tore the place to bits,

the wild, fool ele-
mentals! Gone out now,
leaving their trail, these

tears and from tables
great wine pools dripping
slowly to the floor.

Poem written after contemplating the adverb 'primarily'

This is the room. Those windows
admit swift revolutions
of sunlight, moonlight. So swift they form
the mass. That is the smell. With a spoon
we could not stir it.

The room is called the hub. Hub. There he goes
– those points all equidistant from the churning
(where the darkness
leans all around the wheel, see?) –
the assistant. What he does

we describe as bearding. Notice
his routine. Incessant
innumerable
ingenious ploys hazarded
to attenuate the light (or what

could we be inhabiting?). It is
the same
in each room.
There are many rooms. Each called
the hub.

You should be there when the master comes.
He strides through the thudding diameters.
He reaches the assistant.
He floors the assistant with one blow.
Out he goes again, wearing his old grin.

The assistants are
changed. And the master. The master
with a little
less
frequency.

Three Brixton gardens

In this one a boy
engages brickwork
bouncing a football –

the one-eyed house
has one, the soil just
turned for planting

a prairie, there the boy's
friend saddles up, hugs
a black twister

of hoofs at any sound
of leather
bouncing; in a third

the smell of tea,
the smell of washing make
a bit of a man

happy, happier
without vistas
of wheat or longhorn,

happiest without
the mist and its
immense animals.

Songsheet song about Liebknecht in Brixton

When Liebknecht walked in Brixton
He asked a coloured man:
How long can you live
On bread and jam?

When Liebknecht walked in Brixton
He asked a coloured child:
What happened in school,
Did they say you smelled?

When Liebknecht walked in Brixton
He asked a coloured girl:
Which staff manager said No
Because customers will?

When Liebknecht walked in Brixton
White cabbage vendors grinned:
No flies on that bastard,
Talks them into the ground.

Young woman in apathy

Something, the sandwich and the coffee –
but her look (if you knew) could blind. Soon
something may crack inside it – listen:

over her cup, still as desolate, the misty
ovals make nothing of her trees and men; unholed
ice, and she shooting under the ice out of no-

where; no star (to feed on sandwich), not
a faint star, even, who'll sneak into
averted vision – caryatid! –

what in all the world is company? what is it?
Blood bawling its lies back at an impromptu 'O
I am so unhappy,' or some such? Even 'it's

me' pretends, fools
no one, lets
go the least sound

collapsing the pediment,
and she – suffocated in a heap
under her stone gods.

Generations

On his oblong
blotting pad, indelible,
indecipherable,
a sum short of a total,
the signature doubling back –

In no hand of his, but
his father's, dead: must,
let him conjecture, identity,
here or recollected, come
to this – what sons

at the panicking
from his mouth of a call
or figure would not recoil,
all nerves,
unknowing,

or: older, needled, none
dare read in the mirror what
matter the remote
index of a will
jabbed at, dwelt on.

Never the solar track, merely
its similitudes, a rain of dreams
clubbing the gory hue
into substance, these
puzzled records of his goings-on.

The monsters

They slide from rooms,
trees, tunnels, and gleam
in the airy halls, diffusing
round their bulk the stale
room-stench, tree-glue, tunnel-twinklings.

Bodies, bearable to themselves, chairing it
down the airy corridors, a
mutual shoving, a sedate
crush, happy, crashing the stillness,
bored, they pick

and mull it over in their shaggy
stomachs, the music, as emotion
to be recognized, figuring
its flesh to be
their lightest repast.

A time is coming for the monsters.
They begged their helpings of it,
the music, and we lent them
our ears, played into
their hands our instruments.

In the light

Sitting in the light by the fireplace,
she held her daughter's nightdress up.

It would have fitted a girl of sixteen,
but her daughter is less than half that.

All the same, she said, if the girl wants,
let her wear it – the hem warms her feet!

Then she began to pin a strong patch
across the shoulders of the thing.

When the hem comes up to the knees,
her daughter will think of marriage.

As the feet vanish in it, I enquire: why
start always at nought and move along?

It's the lack of any alternative;
like being born with ten thumbs.

Stony old men, it's no wonder
you kept on willing the utterly other.

Soon made adaptable its cruel machines.
Round whizzing absolutes ranged your needs.

Yet someone here can stitch the garment still;
and it must be evil to forgive such things.

The snowy bed, ha, this dead of winter,
she'll not let little feet go down it bare.

Sitting in the light by the fireplace,
she held up her daughter, the way it is.

Penny pastorals in Texas

1

MUD-DAUBER

On yellow shanks which slot into black thighs,
hoisting his behind he crouches,
nose down, sipping mud.

Look long enough, if you can, to
measure the waist. The wings have spread,
or they fold up for poise.

Somewhere in that machine the grains
of mud get stored, once truly munched.
He licks the rock clean;

then bounces off, as if air were cushions,
hangs dazed, in mid-air, to spy out
some fresh crevice,

drops hard on it, and stoops again, quaking
in the static dive. His flight mimics
the buzzard's drift

along whatever warm current may offer,
over the barnyards and the airports,
creeks and turtle backs;

but is blinder, a black mist solidified
into the floating leggity tube
that lolls as it steers.

Then under eaves he mouths the pulp out,
to the shape his trowel nose and hundred
voyages aimed at.

His colonies cluster; each nest shall hug
its dry egg by October; and the house
must wear that necklace,

while smoke of cedar scents our room,
and we lug by hand strong logs home,
for the few cold days.

2

A bayed wall of red brick,
pillars white and squared;

south a roof like a prairie
schooner balloons and rolls.

Their shrubs lap the pecan shade;
the mechanic plugs in, whistling,

and slopes off, elsewhere.
Grass gnaws old local news,

and four cans decompose,
then across a jack on wheels

an ant headed full pelt
for their torn canyons.

In roasting yards coloured
men hack the hard dirt down

with shovels. But here,
a shelf for the crisps,

and a shelf for the fram,
the sign saying . . . CHARGED,

even coke bottles caught it,
and at shoe height a can's alm

of copper rain had –
not pounding sun but a dense

lustre mounting the spine,
a cool in the body, recoiling

from the same cans, and again –
it was exultation for the way

they came to propose to be,
in a slow regard, so long

the pouring down of air
among minerals had lost cause,

and left none for alarm.
This might be perceived

after forty minutes
of standing still;

for once not able, not
needing, even, to move on.

3

NIGHT SOUND IN JUNE

It begins
at dusk – with a ping
the overbaked
bowl of night begins
to craze,
and a snaky cool –

strongest in the hills,
it may succeed
chuck-will's widow's
rippling treble –
least
explicable its prickling
the foreign ear –

soda sparks
into perpetuity – drummed
phosphorescence
as quartz beams fizz
fork lightning
from their gangue's thick dark
crisscross
through scores of holes –

then to the bleat, shrilled, of lambs
round bronchial ewes
entire kibbutzim of gnomes begin
grinding wee scythes –

midget grannies
knitting on clickety cactus spines
breech clouts for wizen brats
jabber
sforzando snippets of news
and slurp quick
gins without cease –

now dark
chafe dark
fill
night
sightless in
mummystiff
muslin –

Llanorian –

Hermit pot

Down that steep valley, west
of the old town, a brook
threads one plantation.
By peach, bean and marrow,
in that plantation –
bean poles arching over –
an old rotund
earthenware pot is lying.

Passing on down –
it was only the rim shone.
Returning,
it was not there.
Who would have taken thought
of this pot
at that precise moment
as the middle of the enigma of the world.

For a future

Your camping lantern shone among
the cottonwoods. It was then
I should have come. Watching –
the way your lantern swung –
I could have told you from anyone.

Again, now. I shall bar no holds
but surge to you across darkness.
Fluffy as the owls, firm as ready apples,
under your window I shall stand.
Your wall's chimney bricks do for my toes.

It was long ago, in the mountains.
Such deep snow all tracks were gone.
When you slipped I caught you,
pushed you upright with a hand.
Then you were light, and still you are.

The cottonwoods, the antique canyon,
what a place, of tamarisk and sand.
You stood on the sand among rocks,
and stared the sun's way. The truth
was moving so fast I could not stop.

Now there are these cottages, tonight.
Between them, the beans and the cauliflowers
make an odd place, to be sure, for us
together to come to. And perhaps,
after all, it will be too cold,

or our moans will disturb the cows, then
they'd wake the others, coughing;
or the chimney bricks under the appletrees
will not support now the toes unskilled
from being denied you, for so long.

Difficulties of a revisionist

All day fighting for a poem. Fighting against what?
And for what? What? being its own danger, wants
to get rescued, but from its rescuer?

So many voices. So much silence. The air, thickened,
reeks of tobacco, hints of blood; still the thing
gibbering somewhere takes no hints at all.

Up the road in the rain someone stopping a car asks
the way to the next estate. I find myself
giving instructions that will get him lost.

In praise of the functionary

The apple tree cannot trap
his attention. Buds
begin to uncurl; sky,
to turn blue,
liquidates a cloud;
soon fruits evolve,
on long wands flourished
by the bole.

For all that, little he cares.
The apple tree
cannot trap his attention.
He sticks to the bugs,
working madly in the bark,
as usual; to the woman,
darning his sock
at the heel;
to the child or two,
who scream in its shadow.

There are processes which are
not to be bothered with:
these at least illustrate
the effort it takes,
being a bug, darning
a sock, emitting
a scream. Tomorrow he flies
to New York with papers.

neatly typed, important; the sums
are already worked out
in his head. Tuesday
he will convince the steel
collective that the party commands
the wisdom of experience;
that individuals have no
access to this; that errors
must be rooted out.

He builds on dry ground
for us a dwelling.
We thank him that his attention
was not trapped by the apple
tree. Nor by the sea (since
the apple tree only
distracts), the sea
which we behold with wild joy,

also with fear which gnaws
the bones of the bronzed head
he marks human as it steers
a speck through the boiling
salt verticals, the sea
which he ignores
and its crunching
in the bronzed head's
blank marrow.

For a junior school poetry book

The mothers are waiting in the yard.
Here come the children, fresh from school.
The mothers are wearing rumpled skirts.
What prim mouths, what wrinkly cheeks.
The children swirl through the air to them,
trailing satchels and a smell of chalk.

The children are waiting in the yard.
The mothers come stumbling out of school.
The children stare primly at them,
lace their shoes, pat their heads.
The mothers swirl through the air to cars.
The children crossly drive them home.

The mothers are coming.
The children are waiting.
The mothers had eyes that see
boiled eggs, wool, dung and bed.
The children have eyes that saw
owl and mountain and little mole.

Octobers

They watch the big vats bubbling over.
They walk forward, fists dig
into hip bags and sweep in silver arcs
the seed. They put ready
files that will rush from room
to room when the crisis breaks.

They rake the pear leaves into piles
on lawns. Among square mounds
of air bricks they prepare foundations.
They return, with faint tans, to renew
their season tickets. They are giving
again the first of last year's lectures.

They remember Spring. It is the walk
of a woman otherwise quite forgotten.
Wondering if it is for the last time,
they drive through the red forests.
They control the conference tables
with promises of mutual destruction.

They put the cat out with unusual caution.
They clean the flues. They fall
flat on their tough backs off mustangs.
They visit the rice and the apple barns.
They man the devices with fresh crews.
They like the o in the middle of the name.

Celestial déjà vu

(AFTER A POEM BY WILHELM KLEMM)

I woke up to find, if you please,
a horde of pumpkins battering the door.
What sort of a child's was this nightmare?
Their big pot, just who did he think he was?

You should understand:
it was the whole mob. Toad man, jabber man and mushroom,
kicking up such a stink of rostrum,
all quodlibetterers of my mankind!

I might have looked back, for the laugh that comes
when a thing's done with;
but clapped a hand to my mouth –
remembering, so help me, all their names.

Sketch of the old graveyard at Col de Castillon

To get there from here you have to drop
over a dozen or more broken terrace walls;
it is the absorbed oblong far below,
sole plane on the grade of the green mountain.

*

There is no path down to these predictable dead
cabined in their parallels. The way up –
a track rolls off the road, and forgets itself;
antique cars chugged among the grasshoppers once,
or there were twelve shoes to shuffle under each box;
but you arrived jumping, almost out of the sky.

*

Their photos preserve the staring aunt;
grandpapa with a crooked smile like a locust's;
Mimi who looks beautiful and died at 17,
happy in a frock whose narrow V whittles
boneless white to the shape of a weevil's nose.

*

The red-backed grasshopper stuck his head,
shining, through a leaf's hole, shifting it,
little by little, the leaf, beside the blue flower.
Blue flower burying the carpenter bee.

*

The things one imagines of the dead,
who cannot see: broom like green porcupines,
and, higher, the crab-apple tree; cold shrapnel
on the abandoned terraces; the one rose
meandering in through a wire octagon;
and cannot hear the immense murmur now,
floating behind the silence in the air.

*

Oval photo, dryness of the plastic rose;
hollow chapel sprayed with bullet scars.
Picking the father's bones, his flesh

tastes rotten, sticks between the teeth;
different echoes, tomb and the blue flower's bell,
thicken to old screams in the houses you explode.

*

And the marrow starts to itch for the sting.

And the fat daughter wore on her finger
a snail, its body transparent almost,
starry wetness, the knobbed horns taut,
pointing to the rosy mound, the tip of the finger.

Harrar

Dawn, for some reason,
last night, or a sundown,
and it appeared, the house
of Paul Verlaine. In a gray glow,
here was the dockside it stood on.

A room, full of bunks
and benches, then children,
scores of them, women, age,
faces – uncertain. Round their faces,
stolen through a window, light hung.

And a great cry was
gathering itself, ready
to go, pounding my ribs.
Once I turned from the window, said,
inside the cry, 'Whose, whose house is this?'

What else to do with
the cry but help myself.
It was rock. Here they were
with nothing to eat; I was there, having
to eat my rock cry, piece by piece.

The ancestors

When they come, we begin to go;
it's the ancestors,
they walk into the warm rooms,

eye our women and food, hear out
the good words. Then for words
and rooms we no more exist,

once the ancestors have come,
than a little dust on a vase,
than the breath wasted.

How do they come? They make no
parade of moans and winds;
they borrow no fears, none.

I am persuaded they have come
by the strength of shoes,
by the one shirt extra,

but if most by the bloody love
my shoes and my shirt need
to be seen that way,

I tell myself this is a thing
they'd far better not know,
who have lost the knack,

and only accuse, by the malice
they march us out with, from one
to the next lost place.

Old bottles

It must have been long
I lay awake,
listening to the shouts
of children in the wood.
It was no trouble, to be awake;
not to know
if that was what I was.

But I had to buy
old bottles, barter
for steerage, candles too,
each stamped with my name.
It was hurry hurry
racing the factory canal toward
the town of the kangaroo.

Up the street I came
across a knot of dead boys.
In the room with a flying bird
on practising my notes
I found its lingo;
my body knew
those torsions of the cat.

She came by, that girl,
she said it's to you, to you
I tell what they are doing
in South Greece and Germany.
My parents killed, brother gone,
they read this letter, I'll
not be here, you do not understand.

In my striped pyjamas
I was not dressed for the journey.
I changed into padded zip
jacket, boots, canvas trousers,
my pockets bulged with the bottles,
I was carrying the candles,
and I ran and I ran.

Notable antiquities

Cooling
in the Valley of Marvels
I could see the contoured silver

prehistoric disc
of a cloud below, shaping to propel
dews into the faint folds of corn and plum,

and recall how
in Peckham where the beatle boots cost
thirty suppers of frozen cod

and shoppers
happily slice through cars and shocks
of nobody's noise,

was unearthed
some centuries ago
a Janus head, in character notable

considering
the girl's face quarried from curls one way,
the man's hard with a marble beard the other,

is no common alloy
among the models of time
so constituted, hell, the complexion rivals

even the tree
Blake surprised in Peckham, wearing
in lieu of leaves

an angel, it is said –
though how the tree took all this
is nowhere recorded.

Amour fou

The hand taking the hand holds
nothing. And look: the trouble
with two sets of eyes
is that each wants out.

Islands. But we float. If face
to face we sit down in bars,
our space acquires us –
orphans of blue dust.

There is a call for help, milking
an older silence than can give suck.
Me, I shall not resist.
An owl should adore the empty air.

So make your body from the heap
of shadows down my mind. Nothing's there
for you to resist. Today, dear house,
you've not a thing that's mine.

Mirrors – not needed, we
are detached otherwise.
Chairs and shoes, our
dependants – gone.

To the call the one perplexed
voice calling replied less
and less. Darkening our room,
these are the mountains we roll.

Lonely beach woman

TO A PAINTING BY MIRO

This
is Miss Indigo because
HER BONES
unwind
from her navel cone indigo
to her round rib barrel

PUT
round her one two three
stick stars & a cherry
TONGUE
for the sun

her clown's feet upcurling
bananas her INKFISH
head here
jelly holed
by this FOUR-ringed eye &
& a tear-shaped
TEAR
trickles down her neck pin

the stick
stars have come
to HACK
at her the tongue
is hanging by
for a salt LICK

Old man, looking south

Old man, looking south, you saw
these trees with pleasure; from

your toecaps their field began
rolling slopes into the hill behind.

At this gate, you said, I shall hear;
I know quite well when it's coming.

You'd even tell yourself Let's go;
and left the cottage before time.

*

What you saw from this gate was only
oak trees in a hollow. Not a screen:

not the old man, inoperable, mouth
a hole for air to go in and out of.

Not this tortoise mouth of a time,
pulp between the pounding gums;

at best the blades, green and jolly;
perhaps the shell's ambiguous old gleam.

*

Comas of the last years. Once,
sweating and naked, opening the divan

to lay the moon in white linen,
you babbled of love. Whom did you accuse?

And that you should ever refuse to refuse,
benign, some book or the special talk

of work and country people, when the racking
worsened, can make me wonder still.

*

What hosts of things we found to say.
At this gate, looking south, up the hill;

or breakfasts in the Spring, you by then
drinking your eleventh cup of tea.

That was the same pleasure trees gave
or listening, just, for the due sound.

So one day we walked these thirty paces;
you waved and went, not looking round.

Skins and bones

One thing but one
only comes all at once,
and almost came, when,
little red hands,

your tweaks and hits,
husky drummings,
drove to my throat
dark gobs

of blood – more I could
not honestly afford.
All I thought and thought
was Lord, what has living

been anyway, it's too soon,
my hollow clothes! what am I
doing, dying? Now
should I shrink again

to scan so the blank
wall, wishing, too late,
I had known how skins help,
or can, me and these folk

ripen the wiser for living,
I shall try still not to say
O black food, un-
predicted as this afternoon,

you would taste,
had the realities, those,
those, eaten my knowing
bones whole,

the same,
the same,
the same,
the same.

Rentier fantasy

Tonight we shall be content.
An old life is ending.
We and they shall be there,
dancing under the plane trees.
We shall have gone through the gate
of a golden horn and a song.
The horn is gatepost and lintel,
the song in huge foreign letters
opens through the middle.

Shooting bullets, we shall hit nothing.
Buying numbers, ours will be wrong.
We shall be dancing like crazy,
a guitar tune floating the time.
Someone will fall off his chair,
backwards, just from laughing.
The girls with their dark triangles,
tumbled from old broken houses,
will refuse only our money.

Under a silver half moon,
a mountain sky whitening,
the old goat road shall see us home.
In the time to be silent
we shall start remembering.
How much of it all will have gone.
How much that had gone shall return,
hatched into our brilliant new ships, the swoop
of spacious bridges, and cool blue buildings.

Thus

that green
huge wig
sits

vacant
propping
it

inside
must be
trunk

branches
quarts of
sap

glued on
growing
O-

ho this
judge fits
thus

offence
to sen-
tence

Sanity

After bolting my supper,
   eggs, sausages, bacon and chips,
I see this photograph in the paper:
   it is a crowd of ordinary people,
the Jew cocking his thatched head, the old
   vocal woman, the mechanic.

Two hold the middle of the picture:
   a young man, whose face, head-on,
has the symmetry of a dark Ajax;
   a young woman, hair anyhow,
high cheekbones, the lips parting,
   her remote eyes look straight at you.

They are walking beneath many banners.
   These they uphold casually.
The whole crowd is coming at you.
   I walk across the room, for the first time
can raise my face to the black trees,
   a silver sky of Spring.

Dangers of waking

Waking has dangers. When children
stride into the room, one by one, with reports
and messages, you shout and roll over;
but back they come, with more news,
a slamming of doors, a sound of breaking.

Like a friend you meet – what he
confides to you, you, with your empty look,
turn against him: enmity of others
who can confide nothing to anyone.
They were always the aliens,

ignored or savaged by racier children,
regretfully refused a place
in useful professions. Desirable
dead or mute or not at all,
soon every sound they heard,

voices or wheels or waters,
or wind in the barbed wires,
was the sound of a key turning in a lock.
But these dangers of waking –
well, you'll roll over, shout, do nothing,

as when the children strode in,
one by one, like Greek messengers,
to declare the killing of this or that
man, thousand, or million
on the good green sward.

Itinerary for the apparent double

With you the lane winds uphill,
by day, hatching schemes;
by night, cockshut memory overhauls
your brooding mobile mind.

It steepens for you, on splay claws,
feeling the weight of eggs not engendered yet;
up the incline a lost day
floats its faint rose of shadows.

It is dark from the hill's foot to halfway up.
Boys with stones have smashed the bulbs; some shinned
corkscrewing up the posts, to rob them, furtively.
Morgue of maidenhead, *nigredo*, always foots the hill.

Here, for girls, black men come jumping
big from the ditch with naked choppers.
The mewing of owls armours them as they bolt
with goosepimples and their foretaste of moans on beds.

Yet with you the path can be picked out
from the furrow of hushed and curving space
dividing oak bough from oak bough on either side.
On the upturned face a breath of cloud and two stars.

All for you, who edge forward into the dark,
who have no mind to harp on foreterror,
trust these rounds of light, crossribbed by shade,
to be bodies, nameable, loafing against the fence.

Among them you mount the curve to the one lamp.
Here foliage hoards the spray of beams;
myriads of leaves have multiplied occult dawns.
So the beetle steals through moss in the summer night,

locked in his portable house, which he cannot enter,
and is overwhelmed by the cresting forests of chrysoprase.
You'd find it harder going, to their Cold Mountain;
always the snow cone with its ice flanks recedes,

brands in muscle the black joy of the primal motions –
mystery of effort, this seeming barely to move,
till the body, twice-born, swells with tender power,
raging afresh to expel the last stride.

It might be something, to have lived like this,
with a vacant air, behind those blessèd eggs.
Yet you crossed the ridge. You have begun to drop,
free, from the zone of calm that is gorged with nothing.

Or does another day convict by the death of so many,
the slope sucking you under as you run to the choked town,
through shrieks of birds that flash in the sun like axes?
What pain you have to bring, from ignorance, always.

You flail the earth with it, you track the sun's wheel,
either way, up or down, following everywhere the hill;
the child of ashes has it for a spoon;
it domed the round Iberian tomb before Carthage came.

So you are continuous, and might have been noble;
but you will forget and I forget what you have forgotten:
how deep the hill shines under its shade of tall trees,
and when no stars come, goes to them darkly upward.

Crossing

This is the unknown
thing beside us. We
cross the street, walking
together. We walk
across the street,
and this unknown
thing surrounds us.
It happens: to
be saying only what we mean.

Many people are
crowding past us. This
unknown thing surrounded us. Now
it is in us. It must have
claws, for the words
claw their ways from
our bodies. Unless
these are hooks we feel,
this being tenderly
pulled against the huge stream.

We shall ignore it,
this unknown thing. No,
do not give it a thought.
Not now, or it cannot
keep us here, being this way
while we can. Or it may heave
through the crowd,
like a hope,
very destructive
in its ebb from us.

House in the street of doves

So the one room was never opened,
in that house. Someone inside –
a child quietly doing a picture of a house
in the rain; only that
one room led into more never opened rooms filling
the same house.

Also in the room, a table. Through
one thick white wall a window
marvelling at a street of doves. The child put shadows,
two, across the table,
one shadow of a shouldered head, another of hair.
Empty room.

For the child has scratched out the picture;
the child walks across the room
into another, passing through many, in and out,
as if knowing the way,
stopping only a moment by the door which led then
to the street.

From here you could look across, and see
the house. Nobody wants it
now. Down came long demolishing shafts of sun and snow;
but we prudent bugs take
much time over the matter. Our mouths, always busy,
eat things whole.

An Englishman in Texas

FOR DONALD HALL

First he sees the sky. It is the one thing
not making as if to move. Far south
its blue excites the long spine
of hills. To fetch him
home from that higher tangle
could take years.

Coombs below those hills detain him. Sheep jaws
munch on berries which now ripen through
low thickets. A creek appears,
whose yellow weed foam
ephemerids populate.
Limestone belts

polished by bursts of huge rain will occur,
across trails leading him from nowhere
to nowhere. The lizard gapes
beneath a boulder,
and admits, magenta-mouthed,
the baked air

crusting some inveterate scarab. Twirl
of cardinal bird song and blue jay's
retch sculpt on space distincter
verges. Heat becomes
inhabitable, fresh fanned
from their throats.

His haze diminishes, too, when one roof
of rusting tin has topped a hollow,
as if its apparition –
manhandled – had let
at last the estranged eye in
on something.

It hardly exists. Has stuck it out by
a mere stronger irrelevance than
the horned goat skull's candid gaze
levelled at his gaze
across curly miles of scrub.
Prickly pear

looks like a telling friend for time's cripple.
Dwarf cedars thronging undulations
balk grass and buckwheat between
those hills and his place;
so each dawn, like milk, they leave
his new wish

to be present, now, to drop character,
its greed for old presences, its dirt
fruiting demi-selves in groves.
Yet there still he prods
that suture of hill and sky
for ways through . . .

Help him, tall shades, Wallace and Westfall, whose
addresses, inconspicuously,
changed as men flocked round and round
your cockeyed cabins,
bleating and sad, agog at
the gun's wit.

Or do not help him. But let him move once,
free, of himself, into some few things.
Sky, after all, meets nothing.
And with my snake axe
I'll trudge to meet him, should he come
without you.